The Kiltartan History Book

Lady Augusta Gregory

Illustrated by Robert Gregory

DEDICATED AND RECOMMENDED TO THE HISTORY CLASSES
IN THE NEW UNIVERSITY

CONTENTS

The Kiltartan History Book

THE ANCIENT TIMES

"As to the old history of Ireland, the first man ever died in Ireland was Partholan, and he is buried, and his greyhound along with him, at some place in Kerry. The Nemidians came after that and stopped for a while, and then they all died of some disease. And then the Firbolgs came, the best men that ever were in Ireland, and they had no law but love, and there was never such peace and plenty in Ireland. What religion had they? None at all. And there was a low-sized race came that worked the land of Ireland a long time; they had their time like the others. Many would tell you Grania slept under the cromlechs, but I don't believe that, and she a king's daughter. And I don't believe she was handsome either. If she was, why would she have run away? In the old time the people had no envy, and they would be writing down the stories and the songs for one another. But they are too venemous now to do that. And as to the people in the towns, they don't care for such things now, they are too corrupted with drink."

GOBAN, THE BUILDER

"The Goban was the master of sixteen trades. There was no beating him; he had got the gift. He went one time to Quin Abbey when it was building, looking for a job, and the men were going to their dinner, and he had poor clothes, and they began to jibe at him, and the foreman said 'Make now a cat-and-nine-tails while we are at our dinner, if you are any good.' And he took the chisel and cut it in the rough in the stone, a cat with nine tails coming from it, and there it was complete when they came out from their dinner. There was no beating him. He learned no trade, but he was master of sixteen. That is the way, a man that has the gift will get more out of his own brain than another will get through learning. There is many a man without learning will get the better of a college-bred man, and will have better words too. Those that make inventions in these days have the gift, such a man now as Edison, with all he has got out of electricity."

A WITTY WIFE

"The Goban Saor was a mason and a smith, and he could do all things, and he was very witty. He was going from home one time and he said to the wife 'If it is a daughter you have this time I'll kill you when I come back'; for up to that time he had no sons, but only daughters. And it was a daughter she had; but a neighbouring woman had a son at the same time, and they made an exchange to save the life of the Goban's wife. But when the boy began to grow up he had no wit, and the Goban knew by that he was no son of his. That is the reason he wanted a witty wife for him. So there came a girl to the house one day, and the Goban Saor bade her look round at all that was in the room, and he said 'Do you think a couple could get a living out of this?' 'They could not,' she said. So he said she wouldn't do, and he sent her away. Another girl came another day, and he bade her take notice of all that was in the house, and he said 'Do you think could a couple knock a living out of this?' 'They could if they stopped in it,' she said. So he said that girl would do. Then he asked her could she bring a sheepskin to the market and bring back the price of it, and the skin itself as well. She said she could, and she went to the market, and there she pulled off the wool and sold it and brought back the price and the skin as well. Then he asked could she go to the market and not be dressed or undressed. And she went having only one shoe and one stocking on her, so she was neither dressed or undressed. Then he sent her to walk neither on the road or off the road, and she walked on the path beside it. So he said then she would do as a wife for his son."

AN ADVICE SHE GAVE

"One time some great king or lord sent for the Goban to build a *caislean* for him, and the son's wife said to him before he went 'Be always great with the women of the house, and always have a comrade among them.' So when the Goban went there he coaxed one of the women the same as if he was not married. And when the castle was near built, the woman told him the lord was going to play him a trick, and to kill him or shut him up when he had the castle made, the way he would not build one for any-other lord that was as good. And as she said, the lord came and bade the Goban to make a cat and two-tails, for no one could make that but himself, and it was meaning to kill him on it he was. And the Goban said he would do that when he had finished the castle, but he could not finish it without some tool he had left at home. And they must send the lord's son for it— for he said it would not be given to any other one. So the son was sent, and the Goban sent a message to the daughter-in-law that the tool he was wanting was called 'When you open it shut it.' And she was surprised, for there was no such tool in the house; but she guessed by the message what she had to do, and there was a big chest in the house and she set it open. 'Come now,' she said to the young man,' look in the chest and find it for yourself.' And when he looked in she gave him a push forward, and in he went, and she shut the lid on him. She wrote a letter to the lord then, saying he would not get his son back till he had sent her own two men, and they were sent back to her."

SHORTENING THE ROAD

"Himself and his son were walking the road together one day, and the Goban said to the son 'Shorten the road for me.' So the son began to walk fast, thinking that would do it, but the Goban sent him back home when he didn't understand what to do. The next day they were walking again, and the Goban said again to shorten the road for him, and this time he began to run, and the Goban sent him home again. When he went in and told the wife he was sent home the second time, she began to think, and she said, 'When he bids you shorten the road, it is that he wants you to be telling him stories.' For that is what the Goban meant, but it took the daughter-in-law to understand it. And it is what I was saying to that other woman, that if one of ourselves was making a journey, if we had another along with us, it would not seem to be one half as long as if we would be alone. And if that is so with us, it is much more with a stranger, and so I went up the hill with you to shorten the road, telling you that story."

THE GOBAN'S SECRET

"The Goban and his son were seven years building the castle, and they never said a word all that time. And at the end of seven years the son was at the top, and he said 'I hear a cow lowing.' And the Goban said then 'Make all strong below you, for the work is done,' and they went home. The Goban never told the secret of his building, and when he was on the bed dying they wanted to get it from him, and they went in and said 'Claregalway Castle is after falling in the night.' And the Goban said 'How can that be when I put a stone in and a stone out and a stone across.' So then they knew the way he built so well."

THE SCOTCH ROGUE

"One time he was on the road going to the town, and there was a Scotch rogue on the road that was always trying what could he pick off others, and he saw the Connemara man—that was the Goban— had a nice cravat, and he thought he would get a hold of that. So he began talking with him, and he was boasting of all the money he had, and the Goban said whatever it was he had three times as much as it, and he with only thirty pounds in the world. And the Scotch rogue thought he would get some of it from him, and he said he would go to a house in the town, and he gave him some food and some drink there, and the Goban said he would do the same for him on the morrow. So then the Goban went out to three houses, and in each of them he left ten pounds of his thirty pounds, and he told the people in every house what they had to do, and that when he would strike the table with his hat three times they would bring out the money. So then he asked the Scotch rogue into the first house, and ordered every sort of food and drink, ten pounds worth in all. And when they had used all they could of it, he struck with his hat on the table, and the man of the house brought out the ten pounds, and the Goban said 'Keep that to pay what I owe you.' The second day he did the same thing in another house. And in the third house they went to he ordered ten pounds worth of food and drink in the same way. And when the time came to pay, he struck the table with the hat, and there was the money in the hand of the man of the house before them. 'That's a good little caubeen,' said the Scotch rogue, 'when striking it on the table makes all that money appear.' 'It is a wishing hat,' said the Goban; 'anything I wish for I can get as long as I have that.' 'Would you sell it?' said the Scotch rogue. 'I would not,' said the Goban. 'I have another at home, but I wouldn't sell one or the other.' 'You may as well sell it, so long as you have another at home,' said the Scotch rogue. 'What will you give for it?' says the Goban. 'Will you give three hundred pounds for it?' 'I will give that,' says the Scotch rogue, 'when it will bring me all the wealth I wish for.' So he went out and brought the three hundred pound, and gave it to the Goban, and he got the caubeen and went away with it, and it not worth three halfpence. There was no beating the Goban. Wherever he got it, he had got the gift."

THE DANES

"The reason of the wisps and the fires on Saint John's Eve is that one time long ago the Danes came and took the country and conquered it, and they put a soldier to mind every house through the whole country. And at last the people made up their mind that on one night they would kill its soldiers. So they did as they said, and there wasn't one left, and that is why they light the wisps ever since. It was Brian Boroihme was the first to light them. There was not much of an army left to the Danes that time, for he made a great scatter of them. A great man he was, and his own son was as good, that is Murrough. It was the wife brought him to his end, Gormleith. She was for war, and he was all for peace. And he got to be very pious, too pious, and old and she got tired of that."

THE BATTLE OF CLONTARF

"Clontarf was on the head of a game of chess. The generals of the Danes were beaten at it, and they were vexed; and Cennedigh was killed on a hill near Fermoy. He put the Holy Gospels in his breast as a protection, but he was struck through them with a reeking dagger. It was Brodar, that the Brodericks are descended from, that put a dagger through Brian's heart, and he attending to his prayers. What the Danes left in Ireland were hens and weasels. And when the cock crows in the morning the country people will always say 'It is for Denmark they are crowing. Crowing they are to be back in Denmark.'"

THE ENGLISH

"It was a long time after that, the Pope encouraged King Henry to take Ireland. It was for a protection he did it, Henry being of his own religion, and he fearing the Druids or the Danes might invade Ireland."

THE QUEEN OF BREFFNY

"Dervorgilla was a red-haired woman, and it was she put the great curse on Ireland, bringing in the English through MacMurrough, that she went to from O'Rourke. It was to Henry the Second MacMurrough went, and he sent Strongbow, and they stopped in Ireland ever since. But who knows but another race might be worse, such as the Spaniards that were scattered along the whole coast of Connacht at the time of the Armada. And the laws are good enough. I heard it said the English will be dug out of their graves one day for the sake of their law. As to Dervorgilla, she was not brought away by force, she went to MacMurrough herself. For there are men in the world that have a coaxing way, and sometimes women are weak."

KING HENRY VIII.

"Henry the Eighth was crying and roaring and leaping out of the bed for three days and nights before his death. And he died cursing his children, and he that had eight millions when he came to the Throne, coining leather money at the end."

ELIZABETH

"Queen Elizabeth was awful. Beyond everything she was. When she came to the turn she dyed her hair red, and whatever man she had to do with, she sent him to the block in the morning, that he would be able to tell nothing. She had an awful temper. She would throw a knife from the table at the waiting ladies, and if anything vexed her she would maybe work upon the floor. A thousand dresses she left after her. Very superstitious she was. Sure after her death they found a card, the ace of hearts, nailed to her chair under the seat. She thought she would never die while she had it there. And she bought a bracelet from an old woman out in Wales that was over a hundred years. It was superstition made her do that, and they found it after her death tied about her neck."

HER DEATH

"It was a town called Calais brought her to her death, and she lay chained on the floor three days and three nights. The Archbishop was trying to urge her to eat, but she said 'You would not ask me to do it if you knew the way I am,' for nobody could see the chains. After her death they waked her for six days in Whitehall, and there were six ladies sitting beside the body every night. Three coffins were about it, the one nearest the body of lead, and then a wooden one, and a leaden one on the outside. And every night there came from them a great bellow. And the last night there came a bellow that broke the three coffins open, and tore the velvet, and there came out a stench that killed the most of the ladies and a million of the people of London with the plague. Queen Victoria was more honourable than that. It would be hard to beat Queen Elizabeth."

THE TRACE OF CROMWELL

"I'll tell you now about the trace of Cromwell. There was a young lady was married to a gentleman, and she died with her first baby, and she was brought away into a forth by the fairies, the good people, as I suppose. She used to be sitting on the side of it combing her hair, and three times her husband saw her there, but he had not the courage to go and to bring her away. But there was a man of the name of Howley living near the forth, and he went out with his gun one day and he saw her beside the forth, and he brought her away to his house, and a young baby sprang between them at the end of a year. One day the husband was out shooting and he came in upon Howley's land, and when young Howley heard the shooting he rose up and went out and he bade the gentleman to stop, for this was his land. So he stopped, and he said he was weary and thirsty, and he asked could he rest in the house. So young Howley said as long as he asked pardon he had leave to use what he liked. So he came in the house and he sat at the table, and he put his two eyes through the young lady. 'If I didn't see her dead and buried,' he said, 'I'd say that to be my own wife.' 'Oh!' said she, 'so I am your wife, and you are badly worthy of me, and you have the worst courage ever I knew, that you would not come and bring me away out of the forth as young Howley had the courage to bring me,' she said. So then he asked young Howley would he give him back his wife. 'I will give her,' he said, 'but you never will get the child.' So the child was reared, and when he was grown he went travelling up to Dublin. And he was at a hunt, and he lost the top of his boot, and he went into a shoemaker's shop and he gave him half a sovereign for nothing but to put the tip on the boot, for he saw he was poor and had a big family. And more than that, when he was going away he took out three sovereigns and gave them to the blacksmith, and he looked at one of the little chaps, and he said 'That one will be in command of the whole of England.' 'Oh, that cannot be,' said the blacksmith, 'where I am poor and have not the means to do anything for him.' 'It will be as I tell you,' said he, 'and write me out now a docket,' he said, 'that if ever that youngster will come to command Ireland, he will give me a free leg.' So the docket was made out, and he brought it away with him. And sure enough, the shoemaker's son listed, and was put at the head of soldiers, and got the command of England, and came with his soldiers to put down Ireland. And Howley saw them coming and he tied his handkerchief to the top of his stick, and when Cromwell saw that, he halted the army, 'For there is some poor man in distress,' he said. Then Howley showed him the docket his father had written. 'I will do some good thing for you on account of that,' said Cromwell; 'and go now to the top of that high cliff,' he said, 'and I'll give as much land as you can see from it.' And so he did give it to him. It was no wonder Howley to have known the shoemaker's son would be in command and all would happen him, because of his mother that got knowledge in the years she was in the forth. That is the trace of Cromwell. I heard it at a wake, and I would believe it, and if I had time to put my mind to it, and if I was not on the road from Loughrea to Ballyvaughan, I could give you the foundations of it better."

CROMWELL'S LAW

"I'll tell you about Cromwell and the White Friars. There was a White Friar at that time was known to have knowledge, and Cromwell sent word to him to come see him. It was of a Saturday he did that, of an Easter Saturday, but the Friar never came. On the Sunday Cromwell sent for him again, and he didn't come. And on the Monday he sent for him the third time, and he did come. 'Why is it you did not come to me when I sent before?' said Cromwell. 'I'll tell you that,' said the White Friar. 'I didn't come on Saturday,' he said, 'because your passion was on you. And I didn't come on the Sunday,' he said, 'because your passion was not gone down enough, and I thought you would not give me my steps. But I came to-day,' he said, 'because your passion is cool.' When Cromwell heard his answer, 'That is true,' he said, 'and tell me how long my law will last in Ireland.' 'It will last,' says the White Friar, 'till yesterday will come (that was Easter Sunday) the same day as our Lady Day.' Cromwell was satisfied then, and he gave him a free leg, and he went away. And so that law did last till now, and it's well it did, for without that law in the country you wouldn't be safe walking the road having so much as the price of a pint of porter in your pocket."

CROMWELL IN CONNACHT

"Cromwell cleared the road before him. If any great man stood against him he would pull down his castle the same as he pulled down that castle of your own, Ballinamantane, that is down the road. He never got more than two hours sleep or three, or at the most four, but starting up fearing his life would be peppered. There was a word he sounded out to the Catholics, 'To hell or Connacht,' and the reason he did that was that Connacht was burned bare, and he that thought to pass the winter there would get no lodging at all. Himself and his men travelled it, and they never met with anything that had human breath put in it by God till they came to Breffny, and they saw smoke from a chimney, and they surrounded the house and went into it. And what they saw was a skeleton over the fire roasting, and the people of the house picking flesh off it with the bits of a hook. And when they saw that, they left them there. It was a Clare man that burned Connacht so bare; he was worse than Cromwell, and he made a great slaughter in the house of God at Clonmel. The people have it against his family yet, and against the whole County of Clare."

A WORSE THAN CROMWELL

"Cromwell was very bad, but the drink is worse. For a good many that Cromwell killed should go to heaven, but those that are drunken never see heaven. And as to drink, a man that takes the first glass is as quiet and as merry as a pet lamb; and after the second glass he is as knacky as a monkey; and after the third glass he is as ready for battle as a lion; and after the fourth glass he is like a swine as he is. 'I am thirsty' [IRISH: Ta Tart Orm], that was one of our Lord's seven words on the Cross, where he was dry. And a man far off would have given him drink; but there was a drunkard at the foot of the Cross, and he prevented him."

THE BATTLE OF AUGHRIM

"That was a great slaughter at Aughrim. St. Ruth wanted to do all himself, he being a foreigner. He gave no plan of the battle to Sarsfield, but a written command to stop where he was, and Sarsfield knew no more than yourself or myself in the evening before it happened. It was Colonel Merell's wife bade him not go to the battle, where she knew it would go bad with him through a dream. But he said that meant that he would be crowned, and he went out and was killed. That is what the poem says:

> If Caesar listened to Calpurnia's dream
> He had not been by Pompey's statue slain.

All great men gave attention to dreams, though the Church is against them now. It is written in Scripture that Joseph gave attention to his dream. But Colonel Merell did not, and so he went to his death. Aughrim would have been won if it wasn't for the drink. There was too much of it given to the Irish soldiers that day—drink and spies and traitors. The English never won a battle in Ireland in fair fight, but getting spies and setting the people against one another. I saw where Aughrim was fought, and I turned aside from the road to see the tree where St Ruth was killed. The half of it is gone like snuff. That was spies too, a Colonel's daughter that told the English in what place St. Ruth would be washing himself at six o'clock in the morning. And it was there he was shot by one O'Donnell, an Englishman. He shot him from six miles off. The Danes were dancing in the raths around Aughrim the night after the battle. Their ancestors were driven out of Ireland before; and they were glad when they saw those that had put them out put out themselves, and every one of them skivered."

William III

Derry Aughrim Enniskillen and the Boyne.

THE STUARTS

"As to the Stuarts, there are no songs about them and no praises in the West, whatever there may be in the South. Why would there, and they running away and leaving the country the way they did? And what good did they ever do it? James the Second was a coward. Why didn't he go into the thick of the battle like the Prince of Orange? He stopped on a hill three miles away, and rode off to Dublin, bringing the best of his troops with him. There was a lady walking in the street at Dublin when he got there, and he told her the battle was lost, and she said 'Faith you made good haste; you made no delay on the road.' So he said no more after that. The people liked James well enough before he ran; they didn't like him after that."

ANOTHER STORY

"Seumus Salach, Dirty James, it is he brought all down. At the time of the battle there was one of his men said, 'I have my eye cocked, and all the nations will be done away with,' and he pointing his cannon. 'Oh!' said James, 'Don't make a widow of my daughter.' If he didn't say that, the English would have been beat. It was a very poor thing for him to do."

PATRICK SARSFIELD

"Sarsfield was a great general the time he turned the shoes on his horse. The English it was were pursuing him, and he got off and changed the shoes the way when they saw the tracks they would think he went another road. That was a great plan. He got to Limerick then, and he killed thousands of the English. He was a great general."

QUEEN ANNE

"The Georges were fair; they left all to the Government; but Anne was very bad and a tyrant. She tyrannised over the Irish. She died broken-hearted with all the bad things that were going on about her. For Queen Anne was very wicked; oh, very wicked, indeed!"

CAROLAN'S SONG

"Carolan that could play the fiddle and the harp used to be going about with Cahil-a-Corba, that was a tambourine man. But they got tired of one another and parted, and Carolan went to the house of the King of Mayo, and he stopped there, and the King asked him to stop for his lifetime. There came a grand visitor one time, and when he heard Carolan singing and playing and his fine pleasant talk, he asked him to go with him on a visit to Dublin. So Carolan went, and he promised the King of Mayo he would come back at the end of a month. But when he was at the gentleman's house he liked it so well that he stopped a year with him, and it wasn't till the Christmas he came back to Mayo. And when he got there the doors were shut, and the King was at his dinner, and Queen Mary and the three daughters, and he could see them through the windows. But when the King saw him he said he would not let him in. He was vexed with him and angry he had broken his promise and his oath. So Carolan began to give out a song he had made about the King of Mayo and all his family, and he brought Queen Mary into it and the three daughters. Then the Queen asked leave of the King to bring him in, because he made so good a song, but the King would not give in to it. Then Carolan began to draw down the King of Mayo's father and his grandfather into the song. And Queen Mary asked again for forgiveness for him, and the King gave it that time because of the song that had in it the old times, and the old generations went through him. But as to Cahil-a-Corba, he went to another gentleman's house and he stopped too long in it and was driven out. But he came back, having changed his form, that the gentleman did not know him, and he let him in again, and then he was forgiven."

'NINETY-EIGHT

"In the year '98 there were the Yeomanry that were the worst of all. The time Father Murphy was killed there was one of them greased his boots in his heart. There was one of them was called Micky the Devil in Irish; he never went out without the pitchcap and the triangle, and any rebel he would meet he would put gunpowder in his hair and set a light to it. The North Cork Militia were the worst; there are places in Ireland where you would not get a drink of water if they knew you came from Cork. And it was the very same, the North Cork, that went of their own free will to the Boer war, volunteered, asked to go that is. They had the same sting in them always. A great many of them were left dead in that war, and a great many better men than themselves. There was one battle in that war there was no quarter given, the same as Aughrim; and the English would kill the wounded that would be left upon the field of battle. There is no Christianity in war."

DENIS BROWNE

"There is a tree near Denis Browne's house that used to be used for hanging men in the time of '98, he being a great man in that time, and High Sheriff of Mayo, and it is likely the gentlemen were afeared, and that there was bad work at nights. But one night Denis Browne was lying in his bed, and the Lord put it in his mind that there might be false information given against some that were innocent. So he went out and he brought out one of his horses into the lawn before the house, and he shot it dead and left it there. In the morning one of the butlers came up to him and said, 'Did you see that one of your horses was shot in the night?' 'How would I see that?' says he, 'and I not rose up or dressed?' So when he went out they showed him the horse, and he bade the men to bury it, and it wasn't two hours after before two of them came to him. 'We can tell you who it was shot the horse,' they said. 'It was such a one and such a one in the village, that were often heard to speak bad of you. And besides that,' they said, 'we saw them shooting it ourselves.' So the two that gave that false witness were the last two Denis Browne ever hung. He rose out of it after, and washed his hands of it all. And his big house is turned into a convent, and the tree is growing there yet. It is in the time of '98 that happened, a hundred years ago."

THE UNION

"As to the Union, it was bought with titles. Look at the Binghams and the rest, they went to bed nothing, and rose up lords in the morning. The day it was passed Lady Castlereagh was in the House of Parliament, and she turned three colours, and she said to her husband, 'You have passed your treaty, but you have sold your country.' He went and cut his throat after that. And it is what I heard from the old people, there was no priest in Ireland but voted for it, the way they would get better rights, for it was only among poor persons they were going at that time. And it was but at the time of the Parliament leaving College Green they began to wear the

Soutane that they wear now. Up to that it was a bodycoat they wore and knee-breeches. It was their vote sent the Parliament to England, and when there is a row between them or that the people are vexed with the priest, you will hear them saying in the house in Irish 'Bad luck on them, it was they brought misfortune to Ireland.' They wore the Soutane ever since that time."

ROBERT EMMET

"The Government had people bribed to swear against Robert Emmet, and the same men said after, they never saw him till he was in the dock. He might have got away but for his attention to that woman. She went away after with a sea captain. There are some say she gave information. Curran's daughter she was. But I don't know. He made one request, his letters that she wrote to him in the gaol not to be meddled with, but the Government opened them and took the presents she sent in them, and whatever was best of them they kept for themselves. He made the greatest speech from the dock ever was made, and Lord Norbury on the bench, checking and clogging him all the time. Ten hours he was in the dock, and they gave him no more than one dish of water all that time; and they executed him in a hurry, saying it was an attack they feared on the prison. There is no one knows where is his grave."

O'CONNELL'S BIRTH

"O'Connell was a grand man, and whatever cause he took in hand, it was as good as won. But what wonder? He was the gift of God. His father was a rich man, and one day he was out walking he took notice of a house that was being built. Well, a week later he passed by the same place, and he saw the walls of the house were no higher than before. So he asked the reason, and he was told it was a priest that was building it, and he hadn't the money to go on with. So a few days after he went to the priest's house and he asked was that true, and the priest said it was. 'Would you pay back the money to the man that would lend it to you?' says O'Connell. 'I would,' says the priest. So with that O'Connell gave him the money that was wanting—L50—for it was a very grand house. Well, after some time the priest came to O'Connell's house, and he found only the wife at home, so says he, 'I have some money that himself lent me.' But he had never told the wife of what he had done, so she knew nothing

O'CONNELL.

about it, and says she, 'Don't be troubling yourself about it, he'll bestow it on you.' 'Well,' says the priest, I'll go away now and I'll come back again.' So when O'Connell came, the wife told him all that had happened, and how a priest had come saying he owed him money, and how she had said he would bestow it on him. 'Well,' says O'Connell, 'if you said I would bestow it, I will bestow it.' And so he did. Then the priest said, 'Have you any children?' 'Ne'er a child,' said O'Connell. 'Well you will have one,' said he. And that day nine months their young son was born. So what wonder if he was inspired, being, as he was, the Gift of God."

THE TINKER

"O'Connell was a great man. I never saw him, but I heard of his name. One time I saw his picture in a paper, where they were giving out meal, where Mrs. Gaynor's is and I kissed the picture of him. They were laughing at me for doing that, but I had heard of his good name. There was some poor man, a tinker, asked help of him one time in Dublin, and he said, 'I will put you in a place where you will get some good thing.' So he brought him to a lodging in a very grand house and put him in it. And in the morning he began to make saucepans, and he was making them there, and the shopkeeper that owned the house was mad at him to be doing that, and making saucepans in so grand a house, and he wanted to get him out of it, and he gave him a good sum of money to go out. He went back and told that to O'Connell, and O'Connell said, 'Didn't I tell you I would put you in the way to get some good thing?'"

A PRESENT

"There was a gentleman sent him a present one time, and he bade a little lad to bring it to him. Shut up in a box it was, and he bade the boy to give it to himself, and not to open the box. So the little lad brought it to O'Connell to give it to him. 'Let you open it yourself,' says O'Connell. So he opened it, and whatever was in it blew up and made an end of the boy, and it would have been the same with O'Connell if he had opened it."

HIS STRATEGY

"O'Connell was a grand man; the best within the walls of the world. He never led anyone astray. Did you hear that one time he turned the shoes on his horses? There were bad members following him. I cannot say who they were, for I will not tell what I don't know. He got a smith to turn the shoes, and when they came upon his track, he went east and they went west. Parnell was no bad man, but Dan O'Connell's name went up higher in praises."

THE MAN WAS GOING TO BE HANGED

"I saw O'Connell in Galway one time, and I couldn't get anear him. All the nations of the world were gathered there to see him. There were a great many he hung and a great many he got off from death, the dear man. He went into a town one time, and into a hotel, and he asked for his dinner. And he had a frieze dress, for he was very simple, and always a clerk along with him. And when the dinner was served to him, 'Is there no one here,' says he, 'to sit along with me; for it is seldom I ever dined without company.' 'If you think myself good enough to sit with you,' says the man of the hotel, 'I will do it.' So the two of them sat to the dinner together, and O'Connell asked was there any news in the town. 'There is,' says the hotel man, 'there is a man to be hung to-morrow.' 'Oh, my!' says O'Connell, 'what was it he did to deserve that?' 'Himself and another that had been out fowling,' says he, 'and they came in here and they began to dispute, and the one of them killed the other, and he will be hung to-morrow.' 'He will not,' says O'Connell. 'I tell you he will,' says the other, 'for the Judge is come to give the sentence.' Well, O'Connell kept to it that he would not, and they made a bet, and the hotel man bet all he had on the man being hung. In the morning O'Connell was in no hurry out of bed, and when the two of them walked into the Court, the Judge was after giving the sentence, and the man was to be hung. 'Maisead,' says the judge when he saw O'Connell, 'I wish you had been here a half an hour ago, where there is a man going to be hung.' 'He is not,' says O'Connell. 'He is,' says the judge. 'If he is,' says O'Connell, 'that one will never let anyone go living out of his hotel, and he making money out of the hanging.' 'What do you mean saying that?' says the judge. Then O'Connell took the instrument out of his pocket where it was written down all the hotel-keeper had put on the hanging. And when the judge saw that, he set the man free, and he was not hanged."

THE CUP OF THE SASSANACH

"He was over in England one time, and he was brought to a party, and tea was made ready and cups. And as they were sitting at the table, a servant girl that was in it, and that was Irish, came to O'Connell and she said, 'Do you understand Irish?' [IRISH: 'An tuigeann tu Gaedilge, O'Connell?' 'Tuigim,'] says he, 'I understand it.' 'Have a care,' says she, 'for there is in your cup what would poison the whole nation!' 'If that is true, girl, you will get a good fortune,' said he. It was in Irish they said all that, and the people that were in it had no ears. Then O'Connell quenched the candle, and he changed his cup for the cup of the man that was next him. And it was not long till the man fell dead. They were always trying to kill O'Connell, because he was a good man. The Sassanach it was were against him. Terrible wicked they were, and God save us, I believe they are every bit as wicked yet!"

THE THOUSAND FISHERS

"O'Connell came to Galway one time, and he sent for all the trades to come out with the sign of their trade in their hand, and he would see which was the best. And there came ten hundred fishers, having all white flannel clothes and black hats and white scarves about them, and he gave the sway to them. It wasn't a year after that, the half of them were lost, going through the fogs at Newfoundland, where they went for a better way of living."

WHAT THE OLD WOMEN SAW

"The greatest thing I ever saw was O'Connell driving through Gort, very plain, and an oiled cap on him, and having only one horse; and there was no house in Gort without his picture in it." "O'Connell rode up Crow Lane and to Church Street on a single horse, and he stopped there and took a view of Gort." "I saw O'Connell after he left Gort going on the road to Kinvara, and seven horses in the coach—they could not get in the eighth. He stopped, and he was talking to Hickman that was with me. Shiel was in the coach along with him."

O'CONNELL'S HAT

"O'Connell wore his hat in the English House of Commons, what no man but the King can do. He wore it for three days because he had a sore head, and at the end of that they bade him put it off, and he said he would not, where he had worn it three days."

THE CHANGE HE MADE

"O'Connell was a great councillor. At that time if there was a Catholic, no matter how high or great or learned he was, he could not get a place. But if a Protestant came that was a blockhead and ignorant, the place would be open to him. There was a revolution rising because of that, and O'Connell brought it into the House of Commons and got it changed. He was the greatest man ever was in Ireland. He was a very clever lawyer; he would win every case, he would put it so strong and clear and clever. If there were fifteen lawyers against him—five and ten—he would win it against them all, whether the case was bad or good."

THE MAN HE BROUGHT TO JUSTICE

"Corly, that burned his house in Burren, was very bad, and it was O'Connell brought him to the gallows. The only case O'Connell lost was against the Macnamaras, and he told them he would be even with them, and so when Corly, that was a friend of theirs, was brought up he kept his word. There was no doubt about him burning the house, it was to implicate the Hynes he did it, to lay it on them. There was a girl used to go out milking at daybreak, and she awoke, and the moon was shining, and she thought it was day, and got up and looked out, and she saw him doing it."

THE BINDING

"O'Connell was a great man, wide big arms he had. It was he left us the cheap tea; to cheapen it he did, that was at that time a shilling for one bare ounce. His heart is in Rome and his body in Glasnevin. A lovely man, he would put you on your guard; he was for the country, he was all for Ireland."

HIS MONUMENT

"There is a nice monument put up to O'Connell in Ennis, in a corner it is of the middle of a street, and himself high up on it, holding a book. It was a poor shoe-maker set that going. I saw him in Gort one time, a coat of O'Connell's he had that he chanced in some place. Only for him there would be no monument; it was he gathered money for it, and there was none would refuse him."

A PRAISE MADE FOR DANIEL O'CONNELL BY OLD WOMEN AND THEY BEGGING AT THE DOOR

"Dan O'Connell was the best man in the world, and a great man surely; and there could not be better than what O'Connell was.

"It was from him I took the pledge and I a child, and kept it ever after. He would give it to little lads and children, but not to any aged person. Pilot trousers he had and a pilot coat, and a grey and white waistcoat.

"O'Connell was all for the poor. See what he did at Saint Patrick's Island—he cast out every bad thing and every whole thing, to England and to America and to every part. He fought it well for every whole body.

"A splendid monument there is to him in Ennis, and his fine top coat upon him. A lovely man; you'd think he was alive and all, and he having his hat in his hand. Everyone kneels down on the steps of it and says a few prayers and walks away. It is as high as that tree below. If he was in Ireland now the pension would go someway right.

"He was the best and the best to everyone; he got great sway in the town of Gort, and in every other place.

"I suppose he has the same talk always; he is able to do for us now as well as ever he was; surely his mercy and goodness are in the town of Gort.

"He did good in the world while he was alive; he was a great man surely; there couldn't be better in this world I believe, or in the next world; there couldn't be better all over the world.

"He used to go through all nations and to make a fight for the poor; he gave them room to live, and used to fight for them too. There is no doubt at all he did help them, he was well able to do it."

RICHARD SHIEL

"As to Shiel, he was small, dressed very neat, with knee-breeches and a full vest and a long-skirted coat. He had a long nose, and was not much to look at till he began to speak, and then you'd see genius coming out from him. His voice was shrill, and that spoiled his speech sometimes, when he would get excited, and would raise it at the end. But O'Connell's voice you would hear a mile off, and it sounded as if it was coming through honey,"

THE TITHE WAR

"And the Tithes, the tenth of the land that St. Patrick and his Bishops had settled for their own use, it was to Protestants it was given. And there would have been a revolution out of that, but it was done away with, and it is the landlord has to pay it now. The Pope has a great power that is beyond all. There is one day and one minute in the year he has that power if it pleases him to use it. At that minute it runs through all the world, and every priest goes on his knees and the Pope himself is on his knees, and that request cannot be refused, because they are the grand jury of the world before God. A man was talking to me about the burying of the Tithes; up on the top of the Devil's Bit it was, and if you looked around you could see nothing but the police. Then the boys came riding up, and white rods in their hands, and they dug a grave, and the Tithes, some image of them, was buried. It was a wrong thing for one religion to be paying for the board of the clergy of another religion."

THE FIGHT AT CARRICKSHOCK

"The Tithe War, that was the time of the fight at Carrickshock. A narrow passage that was in it, and the people were holding it against the police that came with the Proctor. There was a Captain defending the Proctor that had been through the Battle of Waterloo, and it was the Proctor they fired at, but the Captain fell dead, and fourteen police were killed with him. But the people were beat after, and were brought into court for the trial, and the counsel for the Crown was against them, Dougherty. They were tried in batches, and every batch was condemned, Dougherty speaking out the case against them. But O'Connell, that was at that time at Cork Assizes, heard of it, and he came, and when he got to the door the pony that brought him dropped dead. He came in and he took refreshment—bread and milk—the same as I am after taking now, and he looked up and he said 'That is no law.' Then the judge agreed with him, and he got every one of them off after that; but only for him they would swing. The Tithes were bad, a farmer to have three stacks they's take the one of them. And that was the first time of the hurling matches, to gather the people against the Tithes. But there was hurling in the ancient times in Ireland, and out in Greece, and playing at the ball, and that is what is called the Olympian Games."

THE BIG WIND

"As to the Big Wind, I was on my elder sister's back going to a friend beyond, and when I was coming back it was slacked away, and I was wondering at the holes in the houses." "I was up to twelve year at the time of the Big Wind that was in '39, and I was over at Roxborough with my father that was clearing timber from the road, and your father came out along the road, and he was wild seeing the trees and rocks whipped up into the sky the way they were with the wind. But what was that to the bitter time of the Famine that came after?"

THE FAMINE

"The Famine; there's a long telling in that, it is a thing will be remembered always. That little graveyard above, at that time it was filled full up of bodies; the Union had no way to buy coffins for them. There would be a bag made, and the body put into it, that was all; and the people dying without priest, or bishop, or anything at all. But over in Connemara it was the dogs brought the bodies out of the houses, and asked no leave."

THE CHOLERA

"The cholera was worse again. It came from foreign, and it lasted a couple of years, till God drove it out of the country. It is often I saw a man ploughing the garden in the morning till dinner time, and before evening he would be dead. It was as if on the wind it came, there was no escape from it; on the wind, the same as it would come now and would catch on to pigs. Sheds that would be made out in the haggards to put the sick in, they would turn as black as your coat. There was no one could go near them without he would have a glass of whiskey taken, and he wouldn't like it then."

A LONG REMEMBERING

"The longest thing I remember is the time of the sickness, and my father that was making four straw mats for four brothers that died, and that couldn't afford coffins. The bodies were put in the mats and were tied up in them. And the second thing I remember is the people digging in the stubble after the oats and the wheat; to see would they meet a potato, and sometimes they did, for God sent them there."

THE TERRY ALTS

"The Terry Alts were a bad class; everything you had they'd take from you. It was against herding they began to get the land, the same as at the present time. And women they would take; a man maybe that hadn't a perch of land would go to a rich farmer's house and bring away his daughter. And I, supposing, to have some spite against you, I'd gather a mob and do every bad thing to destroy you. That is the way they were, a bad class and doing bad deeds."

THE '48 TIME

"Thomas Davis was a great man where poetry is concerned, and a better than Thomas Moore. All over Ireland his poetry is, and he would have done other things but that he died young. That was the '48 time. The '48 men were foolish men; they thought to cope with the English Government. They went to O'Connell to get from him all the money he had gathered, for they had it in their head to use that to make a rise against England. But when they asked O'Connell for it he told them there was none of it left, not one penny. Buying estates for his children he used it, and he said he spent it on a monastery. I don't know was he speaking truth. Mahon made a great speech against him, and it preyed on O'Connell, and he left the country and went away and died in some place called Genoa. He was a very ambitious man, like Napoleon. He got Emancipation; but where is the use of that? There's Judge O'Brien, Peter the Packer, was calling out and trying to do away with trial by jury. And he would not be in his office or in his billet if it wasn't for O'Connell. They didn't do much after, where they didn't get the money from O'Connell. And the night they joined under Smith O'Brien they hadn't got their supper. A terrible cold night it was, no one could stand against it. Some bishop came from Dublin, and he told them to go home, for how could they reach with their pikes to the English soldiers that had got muskets. The soldiers came, and there was some firing, and they were all scattered. As to Smith O'Brien, there was ten thousand pounds on his head, and he hid for a while. Then at the last he went into the town of Clonmel, and there was a woman there in the street was a huckster, and he bade her give him up to the Government, for she would never earn money so easy. But for all she was worth she wouldn't do that. So then he went and gave himself up, and he was sent to Australia, and the property was given to his brother."

A THING MITCHELL SAID

"Mitchell was kept in Clonmel gaol two years before he was sent to Australia. He was a Protestant, and a very good man. He said in a speech, where was the use of meetings and of talking? It was with the point of their bayonet the English would have to be driven out of Ireland. It was Mitchell said that."

THE FENIAN RISING

"It was a man from America it came with. There was one Mackie was taken in a publichouse in Cork, and there was a policeman killed in the struggle. Judge O'Hagan was the judge when he was in the dock, and he said, 'Mr. Mackie, I see you are a gentleman and an educated man; and I'm sorry,' he said, 'that you did not read Irish history.' Mackie cried when he heard that, for indeed it was all spies about him, and it was they gave him up."

A GREAT WONDER

"The greatest wonder I ever saw was one time near Kinvara at a
funeral, there came a car along the road and a lady on it having a
plaid cloak, as was the fashion then, and a big hat, and she kept her
head down and never looked at the funeral at all. I wondered at her
when I saw that, and I said to my brother it was a strange thing a
lady to be coming past a funeral and not to look on at it at all. And
who was on the car but O'Gorman Mahon, escaping from the
Government, and dressed up as a lady! He drove to Father Arthur's
house at Kinvara, and there was a boat waiting, and a cousin of my
own in it, to bring him out to a ship, and so he made his escape."

ANOTHER WONDER

"I saw Clerkenwell prison in London broken up in the time of the
Fenians, and every ship and steamer in the whole of the ocean
stopped. The prison was burned down, and all the prisoners
consumed, and seven doctors' shops along with it."

FATHER MATHEW

"Father Mathew was a great man, plump and red in the face. There
couldn't be better than what he was. I knew one Kane in Gort he
gave a medal to, and he kept it seventy years. Kane was a great
totaller, and he wouldn't drink so much as water out of a glass, but
out of a cup; the glass might have been used for porter at some time.
He lost the medal, and was in a great way about it, but he found it
five years after in a dung-heap. A great totaller he was. Them that
took the medal from Father Mathew and that kept it, at their death
they would be buried by men dressed in white clothes."

THE WAR OF THE CRIMEA

"My husband was in the war of the Crimea. It is terrible the
hardships he went through, to be two months without going into a
house, under the snow in trenches. And no food to get, maybe a
biscuit in the day. And there was enough food there, he said, to feed
all Ireland; but bad management, they could not get it. Coffee they
would be given, and they would be cutting a green bramble to strive

to make a fire to boil it. The dead would be buried every morning; a big hole would be dug, and the bodies thrown in, and lime upon them; and some of the bodies would be living when they were buried. My husband used to try to revive them if he saw there was life in them, but other lads wouldn't care—just to put them down and have done. And they were allowed to take nothing—money, gold watches, and the like, all thrown in the ground. Sure they did not care much about such things, they might be lying in the same place themselves to-morrow. But the soldiers would take the money sometimes and put it in their stocking and tie the stocking below the ankle and below the knee. But if the officer knew that, they would be courtmartialed and punished. He got two medals—one from the English and one from the Emperor of Turkey. Fighting for the Queen, and bad pay she gave him. He never knew what was the war for, unless it might be for diminishing the population. We saw in the paper a few years ago there was a great deal of money collected for soldiers that had gone through hardship in the war, and we wrote to the War Office asking some of it for him. But they wrote back that there were so many young men crippled in the Boer war there was nothing to be spared for the old. My husband used to be saying the Queen cared nothing for the army, but that the King, even before he was King, was better to it. But I'm thinking from this out the King will get very few from Ireland for his army."

GARIBALDI

"There was one of my brothers died at Lyons in France. He had a place in Guinness's brewery, and earning L3 10s. a week, and it was the time Garibaldi, you might have heard of, was out fighting. There came a ship to Dublin from France, calling for soldiers, and he threw up his place, and there were many others threw up their place, and they went off, eleven hundred of them, in the French ship, to go fighting for their religion, and a hundred of them never came back. When they landed in France they were made much of and velvet carpets spread before them. But the war was near over then, and when it had ended they were forgotten, and nothing done for them, and he was in poverty at Lyons and died. It was the nuns there wrote a letter in French telling that to my mother." "And Napoleon the Third fought for the Pope in the time of Garibaldi. A great many Irishmen went out at that time, and the half of them never came back. I met with one of them that was in Russell's flour stores, and he said he would never go out again if there were two hundred

Popes. Bad treatment they got—black bread, and the troops in the Vatican well fed; and it wasn't long till Victor Emanuel's troops made a breach in the wall."

THE BUONAPARTES

"Napoleon the Third was not much. He died in England, and was buried in a country church-yard much the same as Kiltartan. But Napoleon the First was a great man; it was given out of him there never would be so great a man again. But he hadn't much education, and his penmanship was bad. Every great man gave in to superstition. He gave into it when he went to ask the gipsy woman to divine, and she told him his fate. Through fire and a rock she said that he would fall. I suppose the rock was St. Helena, and the fire was the fire of Waterloo. Napoleon was the terror of England, and he would have beat the English at Waterloo but for treachery, the treachery of Grouchy. It was, maybe, not his fault he was treacherous, he might be the same as Judas, that had his treachery settled for him four thousand years before his birth. There was a curse on Napoleon the Third because of what Napoleon the First had done against the Church. He took Malta one time and landed there, and by treachery with the knights he robbed a church that was on the shore, and carried away the golden gates. In an ironclad he put them that was belonging to the English, and they sank that very day, and were never got up after, unless it might be by divers. And two Popes he brought into exile. But he was the friend of Ireland, and when he was dying he said that. His heart was smashed, he said, with all the ruling Princes that went against him; and if he had made an attack on Ireland, he said, instead of going to Moscow the time he did, he would have brought England low. And the Prince Imperial was trapped. It was the English brought him out to the war, and that made the nations go against him, and it was an English officer led him into the trap the way he never would come to the Throne."

LOUIS NAPOLEON.

THE ZULU WAR

"I was in the army the time of the Zulu war. Great hardship we got in it and plenty of starvation. It was the Dutch called in the English to help them against the Zulus, that were tricky rogues, and would do no work but to be driving the cattle off the fields. A pound of raw flour we would be given out at seven o'clock in the morning, and some would try to make a cake, and some would put it in a pot with water and be stirring it, and it might be eleven o'clock before you would get what you could eat, and not a bit of meat maybe for two days."

THE YOUNG NAPOLEON

"There was a young Napoleon there, the grandson of Napoleon the First, that was a great man indeed. I was in the island where he was interred; it is a grand place, and what is not natural in those parts, there are two blackthorn bushes growing in it where you go into the place he was buried. And as to that great Napoleon, the fear of him itself was enough to kill people. If he was living till now it is hard to say what way would the world be. It is likely there'd be no English left in it, and it would be all France. The young Napoleon was at the Zulu war was as fine a young man as you'd wish to lay an eye on; six feet four, and shaped to match. As to his death, there was things might have been brought to light, but the enquiry was stopped. There was seven of them went out together, and he was found after, lying dead in the ground, and his top coat spread over him. There came a shower of hailstones that were as large as the top of your finger, and as square as diamonds, and that would enter into your skull. They made out it was to save himself from them that he lay down. But why didn't they lift him in the saddle and bring him along with them? And the bullet was taken out of his head was the same every bit as our bullets; and where would a Zulu get a bullet like that? Very queer it was, and a great deal of talk about it, and in my opinion he was done away with because the English saw the grandfather in him, and thought he would do away with themselves in the time to come. Sure if he spoke to one of them, he would begin to shake before him, officers the same as men. We had often to be laughing seeing that."

PARNELL

"Parnell was a very good man, and a just man, and if he had lived to now, Ireland would be different to what it is. The only thing ever could be said against him was the influence he had with that woman. And how do we know but that was a thing appointed for him by God? Parnell had a back to him, but O'Connell stood alone. He fought a good war in the House of Commons. Parnell did a great deal, getting the land. I often heard he didn't die at all—it was very quick for him to go. I often wondered there were no people smart enough to dig up the coffin and to see what is in it, at night they could do that. No one knows in what soil Robert Emmet was buried, but he was made an end of sure enough. Parnell went through Gort one day, and he called it the fag-end of Ireland, just as Lady Morgan called the North the Athens of Ireland."

MR. GLADSTONE

"Gladstone had the name of being the greatest statesman of England, and he wasn't much after all. At the time of his death he had it on his mind that it was he threw the first stone at Parnell, and he confessed that, and was very sorry for it. But sure there is no one can stand all through. Look at Solomon that had ten hundred wives, and some of them the finest of women, and that spent all the money laid up by Father David. And Gladstone encouraged Garibaldi the time he attacked the Vatican, and gave him arms, Parnell charged him with that one time in the House of Commons, and said he had the documents, and he hadn't a word to say. But he was sorry at Parnell's death, and what was the use of that when they had his heart broke? Parnell did a great deal for the Irish, and they didn't care after; they are the most displeasing people God ever made, unless it might be the ancient Jews."

QUEEN VICTORIA'S RELIGION

"Queen Victoria was loyal and true to the Pope; that is what I was told, and so is Edward the Seventh loyal and true, but he has got something contrary in his body. It is when she was a girl she put on clothes like your own—lady's clothes—and she went to the Pope. Did she turn Catholic? She'd be beheaded if she did; the Government would behead her; it is the Government has power in England."

W. E. GLADSTONE.

HER WISDOM

"As to the last Queen, we thought her bad when we had her, but now we think her good. She was a hard woman, and she did nothing for Ireland in the bad years; but I'll give you the reason she had for that. She had it in her mind always to keep Ireland low, it being the place she mostly got her soldiers. That might not be good for Ireland, but it was good for her own benefit. The time the lads have not a bit to eat, that is the time they will go soldiering."

WAR AND MISERY

"There was war and misery going on all through Victoria's reign. It was the Boer war killed her, she being aged, and seeing all her men going out, and able to do nothing. Ten to one they were against the Boers. That is what killed her. It is a great tribute to the war it did that."

THE PRESENT KING

"The present King is very good. He is a gentleman very fond of visiting, and well pleased with every class of people he will meet."

THE OLD AGE PENSIONS

"The old age pension is very good, and as to taxes, them can't pay it that hasn't it. It is since the Boer War there is coin sent back from Africa every week that is dug from the goldpits out there. That is what the English wanted the time they went to war; they want to close up the minerals for themselves. If it wasn't for the war, that pension would never be given to Ireland. They'd have been driven home by the Boers if it wasn't for the Irish that were in the front of every battle. And the Irish held out better too, they can starve better than the rest, there is more bearing in them. It wasn't till all the Irish were killed that the English took to bribing. Bribed Botha they did with a bag of gold. For all the generals in England that are any good are Irish. Buller was the last they had, and he died. They can find no good generals at all in England, unless they might get them very young."

ANOTHER THOUGHT

"It was old money was in the Treasury idle, and the King and Queen getting old wanted to distribute it in the country it was taken from. But some say it was money belonging to captains and big men that died in the war and left no will after them. Anyway it is likely it will not hold; and it is known that a great many of those that get it die very soon."

A PROPHECY

"It is likely there will be a war at the end of the two thousand, that was always foretold. And I hear the English are making ships that will dive the same as diving ducks under the water. But as to the Irish Americans, they would sweep the entire world; and England is afraid of America, it being a neighbour."

NOTES

I have given this book its name because it is at my own door, in the Barony of Kiltartan, I have heard a great number of the stories from beggars, pipers, travelling men, and such pleasant company. But others I have heard in the Workhouse, or to the north of Galway Bay, in Connemara, or on its southern coast, in Burren. I might, perhaps, better have called the little book Myths in the Making.

A sociable people given to conversation and belief; no books in the house, no history taught in the schools; it is likely that must have been the way of it in old Greece, when the king of highly civilised Crete was turned by tradition into a murderous tyrant owning a monster and a labyrinth. It was the way of it in old France too, one thinks, when Charlemagne's height grew to eight feet, and his years were counted by centuries: "He is three hundred years old, and when will he weary of war?" Anyhow, it has been the way of modern Ireland—the Ireland I know—and when I hear myth turned into history, or history into myth, I see in our stonebreakers and cattle drivers Greek husbandmen or ancient vinedressers of the Loire.

I noticed some time ago, when listening to many legends of the Fianna, that is about Finn, their leader, the most exaggerated of the tales have gathered; and I believe the reason is that he, being the greatest of the "Big Men," the heroic race, has been most often in the mouths of the people. They have talked of him by their fire-sides for two thousand years or so; at first earlier myths gathered around him, and then from time to time any unusual feats of skill or cunning shown off on one or another countryside, till many of the stories make him at the last grotesque, little more than a clown. So in Bible History, while lesser kings keep their dignity, great Solomon's wit is outwitted by the riddles of some countryman; and Lucifer himself, known in Kiltartan as "the proudest of the angels, thinking himself equal with God," has been seen in Sligo rolling down a road in the form of the *Irish Times*. The gods of ancient Ireland have not escaped. Mananaan, Son of the Sea, Rider of the Horses of the Sea, was turned long ago into a juggler doing tricks, and was hunted in the shape of a hare. Brigit, the "Fiery Arrow," the nurse of poets, later a saint and the Foster-mother of Christ, does her healing of the poor in the blessed wells of to-day as "a very civil little fish, very pleasant, wagging its tail."

Giobniu, the divine smith of the old times, made a new sword and a new spear for every one that was broken in the great battle between the gods and the mis-shapen Fomor. "No spearpoint that is made by my hand," he said, "will ever miss its mark; no man it touches will ever taste life again." It was his father who, with a cast of a hatchet, could stop the inflowing of the tide; and it was he himself whose ale gave lasting youth: "No sickness or wasting ever comes on those who drink at Giobniu's Feast." Later he became a saint, a master builder, builder of a house "more shining than a garden; with its stars, with its sun, with its moon." To-day he is known as the builder of the round towers of the early Christian centuries, and of the square castles of the Anglo-Normans. And the stories I have given of him, called as he now is, "the Goban Saor," show that he has fallen still farther in legend from his high origin.

As to O'Connell, perhaps because his name, like that of Finn and the Goban, is much in the mouths of the people, there is something of the absurd already coming into his legend. The stories of him show more than any others how swiftly myths and traditions already in the air may gather around a memory much loved and much spoken of. He died only sixty years ago, and many who have seen and heard him are still living; and yet he has already been given a miraculous birth, and the power of a saint is on its way to him. I have charged my son, and should I live till he comes to sensible years, I will charge my grandson, to keep their ears open to the growth of legend about him who was once my husband's friendly enemy, and afterwards his honoured friend.

I do not take the credit or the discredit of the opinions given by the various speakers, nor do I go bail for the facts; I do but record what is already in "the Book of the People." The history of England and Ireland was shut out of the schools and it became a passion. As to why it was shut out, well, I heard someone whisper "Eugene Aram hid the body away, being no way anxious his scholars should get a sight of it." But this also was said in the barony of Kiltartan.

The illustrations are drawn from some delft figures, ornaments in a Kiltartan house.

A. GREGORY.

COOLE PARK, *November*, 1909.

Lightning Source UK Ltd.
Milton Keynes UK
21 November 2009

146513UK00003B/151/A